50% OF THE TIME
THE RIGHT PERSON FOR THE JOB
MUST BE A WOMAN

I DON'T BELIEVE IN QUOTAS. MY ENTIRE BODY IS MERITOCRATIC. I BELIEVE WE SHOULD FIX THE ROOT CAUSE AS TO WHY THE RIGHT CANDIDATE ISN'T BEING CHOSEN. WOMEN MAKE UP HALF THE POPULATION: 50% OF THE TIME THE RIGHT PERSON FOR THE JOB MUST BE A WOMAN

First published in 2019 by Martin Firrell Company Ltd.
10 Queen Street Place, London EC4R 1AG, United Kingdom.

ISBN 978-1-912622-18-4

Devised and edited by Martin Firrell.
© Copyright Martin Firrell Company 2019.

All rights reserved. No part of this publication may be reproduced, stored in or introduced into a retrieval system, or transmitted, in any form, or by any means (electronic, mechanical, photocopying, recording or otherwise) without the prior written consent of the publisher.

This book is sold subject to the condition that it shall not, by way of trade or otherwise, be lent, re-sold, hired out, or otherwise circulated without the publisher's prior consent in any form of binding or cover other than that in which it is published and without a similar condition including this condition being imposed on the subsequent purchaser.

Text is set in Baskerville, 11pt on 17pt.

Baskerville is a serif typeface designed in 1754 by John Baskerville (1706–1775) in Birmingham, England. Compared to earlier typeface designs, Baskerville increased the contrast between thick and thin strokes. Serifs were made sharper and more tapered, and the axis of rounded letters was placed in a more vertical position. The curved strokes were made more circular in shape, and the characters became more regular.

Baskerville is categorised as a transitional typeface between classical typefaces and high contrast modern faces. Of his own typeface, John Baskerville wrote, 'Having been an early admirer of the beauty of letters, I became insensibly desirous of contributing to the perfection of them. I formed to myself ideas of greater accuracy than had yet appeared, and had endeavoured to produce a set of types according to what I conceived to be their true proportion.'

LIV GARFIELD

Olivia 'Liv' Garfield is a British businesswoman. She is the chief executive of the FTSE 100 water company, Severn Trent, which serves 4.5 million homes and employs 6,500 people.

Liv was raised in Harrogate by parents who ran their own project management and engineering business. She was educated at Birklands Belmont School (now Belmont Grosvenor) in Birstwith, close to Harrogate, followed by the co-educational Bootham School, an independent school in York. As a child she had ambitions to be a Blue Peter presenter and the manager of Everton Football Club.

She read German and French (Modern and Medieval Languages) at the all-female New Hall, Cambridge, now Murray Edwards. On graduating, she spent a year at the British Consulate in Brussels followed by work as a management consultant specialising in communications and high-tech markets.

On 1 April 2011, she was made chief executive of Openreach, then a division of BT. During her tenure she was responsible for overseeing the £2.5 billion rollout of fibre broadband to two-thirds of the UK.

In 2014, Fortune described her as the 14th Most Powerful Woman in EMEA (Europe, Middle East, and Africa). She was appointed chief executive of Severn Trent in April 2014, becoming the youngest ever female CEO of a FTSE 100 company. Liv met her husband, Morgan Garfield, whilst at Cambridge where he was an undergraduate at Fitzwilliam College. They married in 2002 and have two young sons.

On the subject of women CEOs in industry, Liv has said, 'I find it a surprise that I'm still rare. It feels somehow not right.'

TRANSCRIPT

Liv Garfield, CEO Severn Trent, in conversation with public artist Martin Firrell, 3 August 2018.

— Martin Firrell: **When did you first realise there was such a thing as power in the world?**

— **Liv Garfield:** I think you know power exists, at least subliminally, from an early age, but authority was probably easier to see first of all. I think I was clear about authority early on. I had a lovely upbringing but there were moments when I'd cross a line - I was always quite cheeky - and I'd be told off. So I think authority is easier to grasp. It wasn't until my teens that I understood power is different from authority. A couple of things made me realise that. One was changing schools. I moved to a different school and I suddenly realised that influence brings a lot of power. In the new, much larger school, I could see that the power was not held by the people at the top but by others lower down, who were not necessarily the best people but they were the most politically astute. It was the first time I'd ever seen politics in play so that was probably when I did my A-levels.

— **Tell me about being cheeky. Were you a naughty child?**

— No, but I always thought I should be entitled to my views, in much the same way as an adult. I had a very loving, close family and my parents encouraged character. I can always remember they'd be having a dinner party and I'd be on the stairs, meant to be in bed, but I was never a sleeper and I'd chuck in my thoughts halfway through the dinner party. These adults would be debating something and I'd lob in a comment. I can remember going too far one evening and being properly told off. It was rare for my dad to really tell me off. I was always trying to interfere in things by expressing my views.

— **You must have been very smart then, young and smart.**

— I don't know. You don't really have perspective when you're that young but I did know I had strong views. I was the typical offspring of parents who had their own business. We tended to talk more about business as a family. Somebody who works for a large corporation can come home and forget about work. If you own your own business the way my parents did, you never switch off. You're always debating. I can remember being seven or eight and debating what we were going to do about a new client my dad had. Whenever we used to go on holiday, we used drive somewhere nice to go camping but we'd always drive past the campsite because there was a client that dad would wanted to go and see, and check everything was working okay. All of that kind of thing was part of our daily chatter.

— **What was your dad's business?**

— An engineering business. They used to create new

designs for chocolate factories. That was one of my favourites: Terry's chocolates and stuff like that.

— **So you have a tradition of engineering in your family history.**

— I do, right? It's really bonkers that I studied French literature at university. I should have done something much more practical. And then it's funny that I've ended up back in engineering businesses. My dad was a brilliant inspiration in that sense.

— **How many other kids were there at home?**

— I have an older sister and a younger brother. Some people reckon that the middle child occupies a kind of forgotten space. In my case it was the opposite. I reckon the whole family turned in so I was right at the centre of it all. Maybe it's different for different kids but for me, being the middle child was the best space.

— **Was this because you were going off like a rocket in the middle?**

— It's probably true that I was causing them to gravitate towards me. They were trying to escape and I was dragging them back towards me!

— **School and politics: what form did that politics take? Is there an example of the sort of political manoeuvring you encountered?**

— So, for example, the whole business of university selection is a big deal. Our school had a very strong track record of getting kids into their first choice of university. They had very good connections. I was not your natural Oxbridge child. I was probably a bit too flighty sometimes and I think the school had the impression that kids who went to Oxbridge had to be incredibly super zany bright - six As at A-level - that kind of thing - a lot more geeky than I was. So I was not their natural choice. Then I went to see Cambridge and I realised that if I had any chance of getting the school to support me I was going to have to change the impression they had of me. I needed to look much more intellectually committed than I had so far. To get the right letter of recommendation from them, it wouldn't be enough to land the grades. I needed their backing. So I went on a bit of a quest. In the lower sixth form, I didn't mind looking a bit ditsy, that was a bit my brand. But in the upper sixth I had to look as if I had gone through some kind of revelation about committing myself intellectually. That was the way to get the school to really support my aspiration to go to Cambridge.

— **That's very knowing for a seventeen-year-old.**

— Yes, maybe, but I liked people-watching. That's probably one of my hobbies. My mum always reckons that, even as a child, I knew how the school was run. She reckons

I was always aware of what you needed to do and who you needed to talk to. My sister wasn't tuned in the same way. I'd always be the first person to come out and say, 'Oh, that teacher's definitely going,' or, 'I can tell the headmistress looks at them in a funny way.' I always knew, even when I was eight, nine, ten, I knew stuff that I shouldn't know. I didn't really know of course but I felt I knew.

— **Where do you think that came from?**

— My mum's a bit of a people watcher as well so it's almost certainly genetics. Have I ever told you I had a really bad back as a child? I had an injury and it meant that I couldn't go to school regularly for a few years. That's why I love life so much. I spent years in bed and sat on a couch. I had two cracked vertebrae that the doctors couldn't fix. Now I try to cram so much into my life - whenever I go somewhere I want to live and breathe it. I lived through years of not being able to do much. When I did go to school I was always conscious that I had missed a few days. I was always looking to catch up on a subliminal level, as well as catching up with the actual lesson. I think I probably learned to watch people better through that. I can remember watching the staff at hospital appointments and thinking, 'They're going to tell me it's all fine. I'm going to have to judge what's actually going on here through their subliminal interactions.'

— **That's quite tough isn't it?**

— You know what? What doesn't kill you, heals you, right? So if I had not had the bad back, I would probably waste time. I wouldn't do anywhere near as much. I probably wouldn't have done anywhere near as well. It was probably the best thing that happened to me. When I went back to school I wanted to catch up with everything. I didn't just want to do the lessons. I wanted to know who had fallen out with who, which teacher wasn't getting on with which teacher. I think I just wanted to watch the whole world in 3D and Technicolour. Everybody else was probably a bit less obsessed with it because they'd seen it all first time round. I could also see what had changed. It's interesting isn't it? If you step back you can see things more clearly. We say that at work all the time, don't we? That's the real value in non-exec work. I attended school for five years as if I was a non-exec. Everyone else went five days a week and I didn't and I wonder whether that gave me more of an ability to see what was really going on.

— **That's quite Proustian. When Proust was forced to stay inside his cork-lined room and remember everything, he was effectively able to live his life over again.**[1]

— There was a big Hollywood film a few years ago

about this guy who could go back in time. The first couple of times, he chose to go back to big days and big moments but by the end of the film, he realises it's far better simply to relive every day. He relives every day one more time. Because he knows what's going to happen, he can enjoy the second living of the day really well. I've always thought that was very inspiring. You wouldn't go back and change your history but you'd relive it and you'd relive the little things. I thought that was clever. You know you're going to make that bus, or not, so you learn to settle into it. You don't change history, you simply live it differently.

— **It's very Buddhist. Accept whatever comes with equanimity.**

— Yes. It's true.

— **Can I ask you about your trajectory from school, the letter that you had to get for Cambridge, to being here, now, as CEO of Severn Trent?**

— So, these are the big steps along that timeline. I got my grades, went to Cambridge and just loved it. I think I loved the small college atmosphere. I don't know whether I may be better as a big fish in a little pond? That might be true of me, that might be more in my nature. So I loved that. I studied really well, made brilliant mates and met my husband there. So Cambridge was hugely important, that whole journey. I think I'm probably innately loyal. That might be my defining personal characteristic. Once I love somebody, I'm loyal to them forever. I didn't have any idea what I wanted to do with my life. I had no passion. You know some people wake up knowing they want to be a vet. I've never woken up and known anything. I applied for four jobs, all graduate jobs, purely on the basis of which people I liked when I went to their career evenings. I've always believed that I would be able to give my best if I liked the person I was working for. The four jobs were all very different: Ford, Unilever, Proctor and Gamble, and Accenture. I got offered a job by Accenture and I liked the people and loved my time there. I did five years at Accenture and the thing I loved most of all was the people. The thing I didn't love about consulting is that you don't deliver anything. You give an opinion but you don't own anything. Within a few years I was thinking, 'I don't want to spend the rest of my life just giving opinions to people who don't even bother listening to them.' I realised that the vast majority of consultancy opinions just end up on the cutting room floor. It's just like filmmaking, the best bits never see the light of day. It's quite depressing. So I left to go to BT. At the time, BT was a client of mine. They had offered me a few roles and I kept turning them down. Then they offered me the role to grow an organisation of fifty people into an organisation of three hundred people. The great thing about it was that they didn't know what they wanted. I was thinking, 'I'd like that task because that's vague and incomplete.'

I stayed at BT for twelve years and throughout that time, I was never sure if I'd go back to work after I had kids. My mum worked full-time in the end, but she didn't work daytimes for the first few years of my life. I wasn't sure if that was what you were meant to do. You know the 'mum' influence is really strong so I wondered if I would take a few years off as well. I didn't really know. I was never really trying to end up in a senior role because I thought, 'I don't know whether you can be senior and have kids.' I wanted to be a good mum above all else. Then I had the kids and after five months I was really sure, 'I need to go back to work otherwise I'm going to kill somebody!' I went back and did a few more fantastic jobs at BT. Then Ian[2] left and within months I was at Severn Trent. I didn't mean to leave so quickly but when your boss changes, it can cause you to re-think and at the same time people were phoning up offering amazing roles and the Severn Trent one stood out.

— **Tell me more about having kids. Lots of people talk about the balancing act mothers end up having to manage. Do you have two children?**

— Yes, two boys.

— Are they close together in age?

— Twenty-three months

— So you had a baby, did five months at home and thought, 'I have to go back to work.' Then you had another baby quite quickly. You must have been quite confident about making it all work.

— The first child is the game changer. When you have your first child you think, 'Life's never going to be the same again.' It felt quite scary with the second one because I was back at work after five and a half months' maternity leave, and then I thought, 'I need to have another baby now if I want them to be two years apart.' My siblings are two years apart and my husband and his sister are two years apart so it seemed natural to want the same for our family. I was lucky because I worked for a great guy, Ian Livingstone. I went back to BT four days a week. He said, 'I'd rather we agree that you come back full time because I don't ever want to feel guilty about giving you loads of work and at this grade I can't not give you loads of work as you're part of the Operating Committee.[3] But at the same time, I don't care if you don't work Wednesdays. As long as you get everything done, don't work whenever you want. Don't work Tuesdays and Wednesdays if you can manage it but I don't want ever to feel guilty. Make sure you buy child care for five days of the week but it's your choice how you manage it.' If I had had to go back five days a week, I wonder if I would have had the second baby so quickly. Going back four days a week and knowing that I had an amazing nanny (who's still with us ten years on) made a real difference. You can only do this if you've got a really good partner as well. You've got to do your share. For example, Morgan and I have always agreed that one of us does mornings and one of us does evenings. You might trade it between you but in principle I'm meant to be home every night at 6.30pm and in principle he doesn't leave the house every day until 7.45pm. The combination of a fab husband, an amazing nanny and a good boss made it all less scary but I never had a third child and I did intend to. I just couldn't work out when, work-wise, I was meant to fit in a third baby. That's an example, I guess, of compromise. Sometimes I think, 'I wonder if I should have had that third child?' My husband thinks that's a ridiculous idea. He reckons we can't cope with the two we've got, half the time. But you've got to make some compromise. I know some people have four. I don't know how they manage that. Two and a job is about all I can manage.

— **Alex Mahon has four.**

— I really couldn't believe that. I read her bio and I just

thought to myself, 'Wow!'

— But she's so funny. She says that people ask her all the time, in business, 'How do you come to have four children?' And she just says, 'I'm very fertile.' What they really mean is, 'How have you achieved this much professionally and had four children?' She was telling me a story about being in a meeting and there was a man in the same meeting who also had four children but no one asked him how he managed it. Her colleague said, 'Don't you get bored with being asked all the time?'

— Does she?

— She said yes. But then she always says something naughty in response like, 'It's my ovaries,' just to bounce the question back at people in a creative way. If it's not too personal a question, how is family life now? Lots of people talk about balancing work and children. Often they talk about being pulled in several directions at once around work and home and kids.

— When your kids are tiny, the problem is you're broken through lack of sleep. So you're over emotional about it all for the first few years. My kids are now ten and eight which means they think I'm legendary. They're at that great age.

They've not got to the teenage years yet and the angst of that. Smaller kids typically have small problems, right? The size of problem they're going to have on an average evening is bite-sized. Someone might have been nasty to them. They might have hurt their head playing rugby. They might want to go to a birthday party and they've got two invites that clash. They're bite-sized problems, aren't they? What I don't know is how tricky it gets when they get to be teenagers because suddenly they're not bite-sized problems! Just now, this is probably the perfect moment for family, work, kids, home. Small kids, small problems. It's good at the moment, really, really, really good.

— **What about if they get ill with something like the chicken pox?**

— I've still got my full-time nanny. Some people try to save money on it. I've had the same nanny for ten years and she's there. So if it's simple stuff like chicken pox, that's fine. During the night I'll be up doing the bloody calamine lotion and then during the day I'm very pleased to go to work and hand it to Sarah. So that's easy. I think it's tricky when they're injured. One of my boys managed to break his arm three times last year. We had three operations and that was quite stressful. You get a phone call out of the blue. Something's happened. Then there are the operations. But then that's actually more manageable in a way because who cares about work when your child's got a broken limb? When your child's about to be operated on, you really couldn't care less what's happening with work. That's when your senior leadership team step up and everything works. The tricky bit is in between. If your child has an immediate issue like that, it's obvious where your priority is. If they've got something basic like chicken pox it's also obvious where your priority is. I think the trickiest situation is probably when you've got something in between and I've not really had that yet. I've seen friends have situations where it's not clear what's wrong with the child. That is probably the most tricky. I've been lucky.

— **Can I ask you about having power? You clearly do have power.**

— Interesting. I never think of it as power.

— **We had this conversation at dinner,[4] about the idea of 'authority' or 'influence' or 'the ability to lead the team' being more comfortable than the idea of 'power'. Power is an odd word. But you definitely do have power. I remember when we met at Openreach, you told me that the one thing you worried about was the safety of the engineers working at the top of telegraph poles in high winds. That's the responsibility side of power isn't it? You said, 'What**

if someone gets hurt?' That was your concern. That's not about influence and authority. That is about power and responsibility isn't it?

— Yes, but responsibility is very different to power, right? If there is a word that I identify with, it's responsibility. I can worry about stuff like that and that doesn't feel like power. I feel very comfortable with the word 'responsibility' and that actually is the reality. Being the chief executive is all about responsibility, leadership and responsibility. The buck stops with you on everything and your behaviours shape the organisation. Actually you've got a huge responsibility at all times to be almost better than you might naturally want to be. You've got to set that tone and one flippant comment could really change people's lives, so you've got to be very careful. You have a responsibility to do the right thing for capitalism, for the country. That all feels quite different to power. I still struggle with the word 'power'.

— **The word 'power' itself feels gendered to me. The desire for power seems quite male, the idea that 'I'd quite like to have power' as an end in itself. I have heard people say, 'I just want to be important and powerful. It doesn't really matter what sphere.'**

— Yes that's interesting whereas I want to feel like I turn up and I create a better place for everyone to work. I don't want to be powerful.

— **That's quite a motherly idea: create the conditions for people to flourish.**

— The two reasons I come to work are 1.) I think I can make my organisation a better place. I genuinely think I can do that. 2.) I love people so I love knowing and hanging out with people and I do that every day. I couldn't sit in an office and be on my own. That would be horrendous. But equally I love knowing that all those people I touch, I could help them develop their careers.

— **Can we talk about gender a little bit? You've said you never worried too much about it or hadn't felt it was too much of a big deal.**

— I meet lots of people who have found gender a big deal, shaping their careers. It's been less of a deal for me and I think it's partly because I don't see gender. Lots of women say, 'I go into the room of senior leaders and I'm the only woman,' and they really notice it. I just go into the room and see people I like and I don't see the gender. I don't know why I don't see it as much. Occasionally I'll go to a dinner and I'll notice everyone's wearing a bow tie and a black suit. Then I realise it's because everyone's male. But it's more because I've noticed how dark the clothing is than I've noticed everybody's gender. So I see people. I don't see sex.

— I have quite a lot of sympathy for the idea that 'my first thought is, do I like this person? Not how old are they? What gender are they? What colour are they? Decide if you like them or not and then work from there.' But what about people looking at you? Did you ever feel expectations of you were different because of being a woman?

— How do we ever know if it was because I was a woman or because I was young or because I was a bit flighty or whatever? All of those could be true. I'm sure people judged me on the way up. I remember going home one day, when I was something like 25, and saying I had had a dreadful day. I remember my husband saying to me, 'Leadership isn't a popularity contest,' and I thought, 'He's so right!' From then on I thought, 'I'm here to be respected and I've got to make sure that everything I do I can look myself in the eye in the mirror. I've always judged my own conduct on the basis that I would never treat anybody in a manner that I wouldn't be happy for my mum or my sister or my brother to be treated. I assume the positive in everyone even if somebody is being a bit patronising or asks me to pour the coffee. I kind of think, 'It doesn't matter.' I'm not here to make a moment about it, I'm here to make a meeting and it doesn't matter what happens around it, it's about how the actual event plays out. Maybe I've just got a thicker skin and I'm less energised about that stuff.

— **Didn't someone once tell you to cut your hair if you wanted to be taken seriously?**

— Yes. At BT I was told I should cut my hair if I wanted to join the Operating Committee. To be fair, this was before Ian became CEO. They got me a coach who gave me some brilliant advice. She gave me five tips and one of them was: try to look a bit more professional when you turn up. I used to turn up with a carrier bag often, like a Tesco carrier bag, rather than a briefcase. She gave me a bit of feedback on that, which was fair enough, right? She said maybe I could upgrade from the carrier bag. You'll be pleased to know I bought myself a decent handbag. The second piece of advice was that I should get a decent pen. I didn't bother doing that but her point was: just look a bit more mature. It was because I was about 28 at the time and she said, 'You look too young. You look like you're 24 when you're 28. Can you not get glasses and get a haircut and buy some pearls? Her point was really: you need to look older or you need to act a bit older. I was probably a bit flippant and a bit flighty and I probably had my hair in a pony tail and I was probably acting a bit like I was 24. On a piece of paper you can imagine a 'Me Too' campaign moment of 'how they told me to cut my hair' but the advice was actually given in a lovely spirit.

— **It's interesting though, isn't it? Because it does speak of a paradigm, a structure in which the expectation is you mustn't be too flighty or too young because then you're not serious. I think that has changed because of people like Mark Zuckerberg in his hoody.**

— The point is, 20 years ago when the advice was given, it was a bigger deal to 'look corporate'. Now it's okay not to.

— **There was a lot more emphasis on conformity 15, 20 years ago in the whole of society, the idea that, 'you need to conform to a certain set of expectations if you're going to be a nurse or a lawyer etc...'**

— Or a librarian, right? I don't know whether people weren't trying to promote women at the time. I know it's mesmerising that there are still so few women leaders in the FTSE 100. I look at it and wonder whether lots of people just felt that conformity was what was expected of them. And then lost their confidence because of that perceived expectation. I was lucky that my line manager - my boss at the time - was a bit less conformist and I think the combination of those two things was helpful. He was quite conformist himself but didn't demand conformity in his team - so a combination of less conformism from him and a bit of a thicker skin meant that I didn't get put off.

— **You don't come across as thick-skinned. I'd imagine someone thick-skinned seeming very tough. You don't come across that way but nor are you anyone's fool.**

— I'm probably very resilient. Every night I always say to my team, 'However bad the day's been, you know what? The day's done.' The great thing is it's finished now, however difficult it was. We all get to go to bed and when we wake up, it's a different day. Yesterday is gone. It's chip paper and I don't allow myself to get worried about days that went badly or last week's challenges, all right? Today is a fresh day. I wake up every day totally positive that today is going to be amazing.

— **Every day is a new thing, isn't it?**

— If you start smiling, people smile back at you. If you start feeling a bit worried about the day, typically everyone else gets worried about the day and you start to propagate that kind of day.

— **What are your feelings about affirmative action and quotas? Clare Short told me when the Labour Party was trying to bring more women into parliament, it adopted a policy of all-female shortlists.**[5] **She reckoned this worked really well for the Labour Party and got a lot more happening for**

women at grass roots level. It got a lot more women into parliament.

— I don't believe in quotas. I absolutely don't because society should not need quotas to drive it forwards. I'm a massive fan of meritocracy. Suppose the best Prime Minister the UK was destined to have was a man, except he never got selected because of the all-female shortlists? That's what none of us can ever know, right? Whilst affirmative action might be great for women, we might have missed somebody who was meant to lead the nation and could have created a more prosperous future for everyone. I'm all about meritocracy, my entire body is meritocratic. In a situation like that, when you've got lots of candidates, I can understand why it becomes attractive. Really we should fix the root cause as to why the right candidate isn't being chosen. 50% of the time the right candidate must be female because the logic says they must be, right, as half of the country's female. So you're almost not fixing the problem. You're creating a harsh solution and you don't know what you're missing as a consequence. I'm not saying it was necessarily a bad thing for Labour to have done at the time but I do think it's interesting they've never had a female leader. Quotas are a superficial solution and don't fix the inherent negativity that's stopping female candidates coming through in the first place. In my company we've never had quotas and we were placed second in the Hampton-Alexander report[6] last year. If we had a shortlist with no female candidates on it, I'd be amazed. When I arrived here that was a regular occurrence and I used to say, 'That's not logical. You can't be telling me there's nobody worth interviewing who's female, who's from a different ethnic background, who identifies as LGBT+?' Bonkers right? So we took all gender and all background information off the screening. We do blank interview screening so the shortlist is based on no knowledge of the candidate other than his, her or their abilities.

— **So it's literally blind compiling.**

— Yes it is. We always blind screen in the early phases of recruitment.

— **There are a few studies where the same PhD paper received a higher mark when the candidate's name was gendered male, and a lower score when the name was gendered female.**

— At university, my husband wasn't a terribly hard worker but he got enough points in his second year to get a First. His tutor said, 'I've decided to raise the requirements for a First because I don't think you embody the type of person who has put in enough work to warrant one.' That's fascinating isn't it? They thought it would inspire him to work harder the following year. The idea was that he'd then give more to his studies and they'd give him the First. They just didn't get my husband. He deliberately worked just hard enough to secure a 2.1 because his view was: 'The First shouldn't be dependent on how many hours I've put in, it should be based on my intellectual ability.' They demotivated him totally. They hadn't understood his particular psyche.

— **Can we talk a little bit about the Annie Besant text I sent you? In particular, I was really struck by her comments on women and the vote. She says the argument against women's suffrage goes like this: women can't have the vote because they're not logical, they're all about bias and prejudice. Then she says, 'But by the way we're asking for the vote, we are illustrating our logic, our ability to see the whole picture and it's the responses from men that are illogical, emotional.'**

— I think that whole text is incredible because you could fast forward and debate how much of what Besant wrote is still true today. It's incredible that a hundred years on, we're still having the same debate. Philip Hammond gave an interview recently. The conversation turned to the lack of women on the boards of UK companies. He quoted one board director as saying, 'Every board has to consider very complex arguments and women wouldn't understand the complexity of those business arguments.' That is so similar to the Annie Besant text, it's incredible.

— **It's astonishing that someone thinks that's all right to say. Obviously they think it's true.**

— They probably think it's fine to say because they believe it's a fact. In their mind it's a simple fact.

— **Do you ever feel angry that it's still taking so long and it's still incredibly unequal for the majority of women? Women are still not being treated fairly.**

— I'm not sure anger's ever a good trait in life. I'm not sure when anger's ever helped. For me, the answer is to keep role-modelling. We've made more progress in ten years than in maybe a hundred. I'm a glass-half-full soul. I think to myself, 'I don't know why we didn't make progress for ninety years but we have made some pretty significant progress in the last ten years.' If we can maintain this rate of progress, we'll get there in the end. Once you've got some momentum, that momentum grows.

— **It's like a dam, isn't it? First you get a little trickle of water but then the dam is breached, and the water starts to flow more rapidly. There's a really interesting fact that LGBT+ people perform better in interviews when they're interviewed by women.**

— Is that true?

— **One study concludes that LGBT+ people perform better because they feel less worried about homophobia if the interviewer is a woman. Women in positions of power seem to facilitate greater diversity naturally.**

— That's incredible but isn't it also awful? I find homophobia absolutely horrendous.

— **There's still a lot of the UK where it's difficult to be openly LGBT+. It's all right if you live in Soho, but that will give you a rose-tinted view of what it's like elsewhere. I read an article that suggested walking hand-in-hand with your husband in Soho is not making a statement at all. Try doing the same in small-town Britain on a Saturday night after the pubs have closed and then it's a courageous political act. Outsidership inevitably creates the sense of vulnerability. Sometimes the physical threat is real. During the course of conversations like this, I've noticed that a lot of women live with a constant sense of danger from men. I was reflecting on some of the things women seem to put up with and I thought, 'Maybe if you're worried about dramatic consequences like losing your job, falling into** poverty, being on the receiving end of physical violence, then those things mitigate against women taking a stand for their own rights. Losing your job at the behest of a man because you have stood up for yourself is a form of violence. I wonder about that, about men's physicality…

— I've never seen that so can't relate to that.

— **Well that's great of course. That's the society we want.**

— Well it is, but I generally can't relate to that at all.

— **Which is great on a personal note.**

— I'm going to watch for that, right, at work.

— **Can I ask you about types of leadership? It seemed to me there is a very conventional 'man' way of doing things. This approach is cruder - I can't think of the right word - basic, crude. It depends on giving instructions, telling people what to do. Everything's quite black and white. It's authority based on control. And then there's another way of using influence, authority and power which is about hearing things. It's also about being open to hearing things that are difficult and not feeling that one's authority is being challenged when dissent is expressed.**

— So I definitely believe there are two different types of leadership. I don't know whether they are inherently gendered. I can think of female leaders who behave in exactly the way you described up front. I think some female leaders think they have to. You know, this footsteps thing is quite important - whose footsteps are you following in? They might have followed a very strong male leader and seen that kind of behaviour producing results. What I get excited about is the next generation of female leaders who will make their own mark and won't feel the need to follow old models. I think in my generation of female leaders, you could argue it's fifty-fifty. Half of them are creating leadership in a more modern way. There is a new form of leadership where power feels more shared. I like to believe that there are both men and women adopting that approach. I like to believe there is a fresh form of modern leadership emerging.

— **I think the whole point of looking to women and saying, 'Look, leadership can be different,' is that the example can apply to men too. Men can lead in enlightened ways too. But perhaps modern female leaders are the most obviously different. It's easier to say, 'Look at this example,' because it looks counter-category. A lot of younger men have a different world view about what they want, how they**

would like to enact leadership, the way responsibility sits with them more vividly than any sense of power. We're probably talking about emotional intelligence which I know is a bit of a hackneyed phrase.

— Yes, but I still think it's the best wording we've got.

— **Artificial intelligence is on the horizon and we're going to have to be very smart about how we arrange society when people don't need to work anymore, or there's no work for them.**

— Of course people will still have to work. AI isn't going to take all the jobs. Even in the best sectors, they reckon in fifty years AI will only do 50% of the work. I'm afraid we're still going to have to work, there's no getting away from that. My kids keep getting obsessed with AI and I say, 'Look at the stats right? You're still going to be working. You're not going to be leading a bunch of robots - just get yourself ready for work!

— **And what do you hope for in the future, Liv?**

— I'd like us to live in a meritocracy where the best talent gets on. I'd like to think the future's going to be happier. I think business has become happier but I think it's also become more stressed. The irony, right? When you look at the mental health stats, technology has helped massively in allowing people to lead different lives. But it also means that we're 'on'

24/7. We're going to have to deal with that. How we manage that world, created by technology, worries me for the next generation. And I like to think that we're going to use the power of technology to do the jobs that just aren't that rewarding. There are lots of jobs in the UK that aren't particularly rewarding for the people who do them. I'd like to think we can get rid of all the gunf work and put people into work that is exciting and more creative. I'd like to think that work is going to get more creative.

— **And therefore more fulfilling.**

— Yes.

— **If you let people do things that they find fulfilling, then they can contribute that to society and society gets richer, in the fullest sense.**

— Exactly, business is going to have to become less capitalist. It's going to have to think much longer term and more responsibly.

— **That's the other truth, isn't it, that everything that happens in The City is very short term?**

— Not everything. Lots of businesses are run for a 30-year journey. We just tend to talk about the next three months, right? There are lots of really good examples of businesses run for the long term. I also think there are lots of really bad examples of businesses that are run for the short term. But the point is we tend to hear more in the press about the negatives. I think every business has got to begin to be run with that responsible business kitemark.

— **Thirty years used to sound like an age to me and now it doesn't seem like such a long time at all.**

— Yes, I agree.

ANNIE BESANT

ANNIE BESANT

Annie Besant (née Wood, 1847-1933) was a British socialist, theosophist,[7] women's rights activist, writer, orator, educationist, and philanthropist. Regarded as a champion of human freedom, she was an ardent supporter of both Irish and Indian self-rule.[8] She was a prolific author, writing over 300 books and pamphlets. As an educationist, her contributions included the founding of the Banaras Hindu University in India.[9]

In 1867, she married Frank Besant, a clergyman, and the couple had two children. However, Annie's increasingly unconventional religious views led to their legal separation in 1873. She went on to become a prominent speaker for the National Secular Society,[10] as well as a writer, and a close friend of the society's founder, Charles Bradlaugh. In 1877 they were prosecuted for publishing *Fruits of Philosophy*,[11] a book by the American birth-control campaigner Charles Knowlton. It claimed that working-class families could never be happy until they were able to decide how many children they wanted. It also suggested ways to limit the size of their families. The scandal made them famous, and Bradlaugh was subsequently elected MP for Northampton in 1880.

Annie Besant became involved with the union movement, helping to organise the London matchgirls' strike of 1888.[12] She was a leading speaker for both the Fabian

Society[13] and the Marxist Social Democratic Federation.[14] She was also elected to the London School Board for Tower Hamlets, topping the poll, even though few women were entitled to vote at that time.

In 1890, Besant met Helena Blavatsky[15], and over the next few years her interest in theosophy grew, whilst her interest in secular matters waned. She became a member of the Theosophical Society and a prominent lecturer on the subject. As part of her theosophy-related work, she travelled to India. In 1898 she helped establish the Central Hindu School,[16] and in 1922 she helped establish the Hyderabad (Sind) National Collegiate Board[17] in Mumbai, India. In 1902, she established the first overseas Lodge of the International Order of Co-Freemasonry, *Le Droit Humain*.[18] In 1907 she became president of the Theosophical Society, whose international headquarters were, by then, located in Adyar, Chennai.

Annie Besant became involved in politics in India, joining the Indian National Congress. When World War I broke out in 1914, she helped launch the Home Rule League[19] to campaign for democracy in India, and dominion status within the British Empire. This led to her election as president of the India National Congress, in late 1917. In the late 1920s, Besant travelled to the United States with her protégé and adopted son Jiddu Krishnamurti, who she claimed was the new Messiah and incarnation of Buddha. After the war, she continued to campaign for Indian independence and for the causes of theosophy, until her death in 1933.

ON THE POLITICAL STATUS OF WOMEN

A lecture by Annie Besant for
the National Secular Society
London, 1874

When I was asked to give a lecture in this hall, I hesitated a little what to select for the subject of it. Various reasons seemed to restrict my choice to some political theme, but even with this restriction the field was a very wide one. But it so happened that this was my first lecture in any public hall, and a feeling of loyalty to my own sex made me determine that my first speech should be dedicated to the assertion of its rights; and I, therefore, chose as my subject, 'The Political Status of Women'. I am anxious that it should be clearly understood that I do not stand here as the representative of any society, nor am I even a member of any; therefore, whatever blame may be found with what I say, that blame should justly be levelled at myself alone, and not at the cause for which I plead. There will probably be a debate following the lecture, and in order that both friends and opponents may have every facility for reference both for attack and for defence, I divide what I have to say under distinct headings, choosing as these headings the arguments I desire to destroy:

Why should the political incompetency of women receive so much attention when more pressing wrongs require a remedy?

Women are naturally unfit for the proper exercise of the franchise.

They are indifferent about the matter.

They are sufficiently represented as it is.

Political power would withdraw them from their proper sphere, and would be a source of domestic annoyance.

Lastly (as we have been told so often in Parliament), Women are commanded in the Bible to keep silence, and to be as generally unobtrusive as possible.

It can scarcely be necessary for me to clear my way by proving to you that there are such things as rights. 'Every great truth,' it has been said, 'must travel through three stages of public opinion: men will say of it, first, that it is not true; secondly, that it is contrary to religion; lastly, that every one knew it already.' The 'rights of man' have battled through these first two stages, and have reached the third; they have been denounced as a lie, subversive of all government; they have been anathematised as a heresy, to be abhorred of all faithful Christians; but now every one has always known that men have rights, it is a perfect truism. These rights do not rest on the charter of a higher authority; they are not privileges held at the favour of a superior; they have their root in the nature of man; they are his by Divine - that is to say, by natural - right. Kings, presidents, governments, draw their authority from the will of the people; the people draw their authority from themselves.

It is quite a new idea to the general public that women have any rights at all; duties? ay, plenty of them, with sharp penalties for their non-fulfilment. Wrongs? ay, plenty of them, too - wrongs which will not be borne much longer. Privileges? yes, if we will take them as privileges, and own that we hold them at the will of our masters; but rights? The assertion was at first met with laughter, that was only not indignant, because it was too contemptuous. Our truth is as yet in its infancy - first, it is not true; secondly, it is contrary to religion. The matter is taken a little more seriously now; men begin to fancy that these absurd women are really in earnest, and they condescend to use a little argument, and to administer a little 'soothing syrup' to these fractious children. Gentle remonstrance takes the place of laughter, and thus we arrive at my first heading. *Surely there are more pressing female wrongs to attend to than the question of political incapacity.*

It is perfectly true that the want of representation in Parliament is not, in itself, a grave injury. In itself, I say, it is of secondary importance; its gravity consists in what it involves. You do not value money for its own sake - those little yellow counters are not intrinsically beautiful, nor are they in themselves worth toil, and trouble, and danger; but you value them for what they represent; and thus we value a vote, as means to an end. In a free country, a vote means power. When a man is a voter, his wishes must be taken into consideration; he counts as one in an election - his opinion influences the return. When the working-classes wished to alter laws which pressed hardly on them, they agitated for Parliamentary reform. What folly! what waste of time! what throwing away of strength and energy! how unpractical! Why agitate for an extension of the franchise, when so many social burdens require to be lightened? Why? Because they knew that when they won the franchise they could trust to themselves to remedy these social anomalies - when they had votes, they could make these questions the test of the fitness or unfitness of a candidate for Parliament. Non-voters, they could only ask for reform; voters, they could command it. And this is the answer of women to those who urge on them that they should turn their attention to practical matters, and leave off this agitation about the franchise. We shall do nothing so foolish. True, certain laws press hardly on us; but we are not going now to agitate for the repeal of these laws one by one. We might agitate for a very long time before we gained attention. We prefer going to the root of the matter at once. We will win the right of representation in Parliament, and when we have won that, these laws will be altered. Ten years after women become voters, there will be some erasures in the Statute Book. There will no longer be a law that women, on marriage, become paupers, unless steps are taken beforehand to prevent it; marriage will have ceased to bring with it these disabilities. There will no longer be a law which gives to the father despotic authority over the fate of the child; which enables the father to take the child from the mother's arms, and give it into the charge of some other woman; which makes even the dead father able to withhold the child from the living mother. There will no longer be a law which sanctions the consignment of thousands of women to misery and despair, in order that men's lives may be made more safely luxurious, and their homes, when they choose to make them, kept more pure. The laws whose action is more and more driving women (in the large towns especially) to prefer unlegalised marriages to the bonds of legal matrimony, will have vanished, to the purifying of society and the increased happiness of both men and women. The possession of a vote, by giving women a share in the power of the State, will also make them more respected. Hitherto, law, declaring women to be weak, has carefully put all advantages into the hands of those who are already the powerful. Instead of guarding and strengthening the feeble, it has bound them hand and foot, and laid them helpless at the feet of the strong. To him that hath, it has indeed been given; and from her that hath not, has been taken away even the protection she might have had.

Women are naturally unfit for the proper exercise of the franchise. It has been remarked, more than once, that in this contest about the voting of women, men and women have exchanged their characteristics. Women appeal to reason, men to instincts; women rely on logic, men on assumptions; women are swayed by facts, men by prejudices. To all our arguments, to all our reasoning, men answer, 'It is unfeminine - it is contrary to nature.' If we press them, How and why? we are only met with a re-assertion of the maxim. I am afraid that we women sadly lack the power of seeing differences. It is unfeminine to be a doctor, but feminine to be a nurse. It is unfeminine to mix drugs, but feminine to administer them. It is unfeminine to study political economy, but feminine to train the future Statesmen. It is unfeminine to study sanitary laws, but feminine to regulate the atmosphere of the nursery, whose wholesomeness depends on those laws. It is unfeminine to mingle with men at the polling-booth, but feminine to labour among them in the field and the factories. In a word, it is unfeminine to know how to do a thing, and to do it comprehendingly, wisely, and well; it is feminine to do things of whose laws and principles we know absolutely nothing, and to do them ignorantly, foolishly, and badly. We do not see things in this light. I suppose it is because we, as women, have 'the poetical power of seeing resemblances,' but lack the 'philosophical power of seeing differences.' We must, however, analyse this natural inferiority of women; it is shown, we are told, in their mental weakness, their susceptibility to influence, their unbusiness-like habits. If this natural mental inferiority of women be a fact, one cannot but wonder how nature has managed to make so many mistakes. Mary Somerville,[20] Mrs. Lewes (better known as George Eliot),[21] Frances Power Cobbe[22], Harriet Martineau,[23] were made, I suppose, when nature was asleep. They certainly show no signs of the properly-constituted feminine intellect. But allowing that these women are inferior in mental power to the uneducated artisan and petty farmer, may I ask why that should be a political disqualification? I never remember hearing it urged that the franchise should only be conferred on men of genius, or of great intellectual attainments. Even the idea of an educational franchise was sneered at, low as was the proposed standard of education. When a law is made which restricts the franchise to those who rise above a certain mental level, the talk about mental inferiority will become reasonable and pertinent; but when that law is passed, I fear that nature will not be found to have been sufficiently careful of the male interest to have placed all men above the level, and all women below it. Susceptibility to influence is an argument that also goes too far. I am afraid that people's opinions are but rarely 'opinions' at all. They are simply their neighbours' thoughts covered over with a film of personal prejudice. It is, however, a new idea in England that a class liable to be unduly influenced, should be disfranchised; the Ballot Act lately passed was, I always understood, specially designed to protect the weak from the pressure of the strong. Oliver Cromwell said that it was unjust to deprive any one of a natural right on the plea that were it given it would be abused. Not so; 'when he hath abused it, judge.' Business incapacity may, or may not, exist on the part of women; it is difficult to judge what power a person may have when he is never permitted to exercise it. Tie up a man's hands, and then sneer that he has no aptitude for writing; or, chain his feet, and show his natural incapacity for walking. John Stuart Mill[24] has remarked: 'The ladies of reigning families are the only women who are allowed the same range of interests and freedom of development as men, and it is precisely in their case that there is not found to be any inferiority. Exactly where and in proportion as woman's capacities for government have been tried, in that proportion have they been found adequate.' In France, at the present day, the women rule business matters more than do the men, and the business capacity of Frenchwomen is a matter of notoriety. Lastly, I would urge on those who believe in women's natural inferiority, why, in the name of common sense, are you so terribly afraid of putting your theory to the proof? Open to women the learned professions; unlock the gates which bar her out from your mental strifes; give her no favour, no special advantages; let her race you on even terms. She must fail, if nature be against her - she must be beaten, if nature has incapacitated her for the struggle. Why do you fear to let her challenge you, if she is weighted not only with the transmitted effects of long centuries of inferiority, but is also bound with nature's iron chain? Try. If you are so sure about nature's verdict, do not fear her arbitration; but if you shrink from our rivalry, we must believe that you feel our equality, and, to cover your own doubts of your superiority, you prattle about our feebleness.

Women are indifferent about the possession of the franchise. If this is altogether true, it is very odd that there should be so much agitation going on upon the subject. But I am quite willing to grant that the mass of women are indifferent about the matter. Alas! it has always been so. Those who stand up to champion an oppressed class do not look for gratitude from those for whom they labour. It is the bitterest curse of oppression that it crushes out in the breast of the oppressed the very wish to be free. A man once spent long years in the Bastille;[25] shut up in his youth, old age found him still in his dungeon. The people assailed the prison, and, among others, this prisoner was set free; but the sunshine was agony to the eyes long accustomed to the darkness, and the fresh stir of life was as thunder to the ears accustomed to the silence of the dungeon; the prisoner pleaded to be kept a prisoner still. Was his action a proof that freedom is not fair? The slaves, after generations of bondage, were willing to remain slaves where their masters were kind and good. Is this a proof that liberty is not the birthright of a man? And this rule holds good in all, and not only in the extreme, cases I have cited. Habit, custom, make hard things easy. If a woman is educated to regard man as her natural lord, she will do so. If the man to whom her lot falls is kind to her, she will be contented; if he is unkind, she will be unhappy - but, unless she be an exceptional character, she will not think of resistance. But women are now beginning to think of resistance; a deep, low, murmuring is going on, suppressed as yet, but daily growing in intensity; and such a murmur has always been the herald of revolt. Further, do men think of what they are doing when they taunt the present agitators with the indifference shown by women? They are, in effect, telling us, that if we are in earnest in this matter, we must force it on their attention; we must agitate till every home in England rings with the subject; we must agitate till mass meetings in every town compel them to hear us; we must agitate till every woman has our arguments at her fingers' ends. Ah! you are not wise to throw in our teeth the indifference of women. You are stinging us into a determination that this indifference shall not last; you are nerving us to a struggle which will be fiercer than you dream; you are forcing us into an agitation which will convulse the State. You dare to make indifference a plea for injustice? Very well; then the indifference shall soon be a thing of the past. You have as yet the frivolous, the childish, the thoughtless on your side; but the cream of womanhood is against you. We will educate women to reason and to think, and then the mass will only want a leader.

Women are sufficiently represented as it is. By whom? by those whose interests lie in keeping them in subjection. So the masters told the workmen: 'We represent you; we take care of your interests.' The workmen answered: 'We prefer to represent ourselves; we like to have our interests guarded by our own hands.' And such is our answer to our 'representatives'. We don't agree with some of your views; we don't like some of your laws; we object to some of your theories for us. You do not really represent us at all; what you represent is your own interests, which, in many cases, touch ours. The laws you pass are passed in the interest of men, and not of women; and naturally so, for you are made legislators by men, and not by women. There are a few rare cases where men are really the representatives of women. John Stuart Mill - now dead, alas! - noblest and most candid of philosophers and Statesmen; Professor Fawcett,[26] a future leader; Jacob Bright,[27] our steadfast friend: these, and a few others, might fairly be called representatives of women in Parliament. Outside the House, too, we have a few gallant champions, pre-eminent among whom is Moncure Conway,[28] whose voice is always raised on the side of freedom and justice. But what we demand is the right to choose our own representatives, so that our voice may have its share in making the laws which we are bound to obey. We share the duty of supporting the State, and we claim the right of helping to guide it. Taxation and representation run side by side, and if you will not allow us to be represented, you have no right to tax us. I may suggest here, in reference to the contest about married women having votes, that this point is altogether foreign to the discussion. The right to a vote and the qualification for a vote, are two distinct things, and come under different laws. The one is settled by Act of Parliament, the other by the revising barrister. A blunder was lately made by putting into a Bill a special disqualification of married women. Such a clause is absurdly out of place. We are contending to remove from a whole sex a legal disability; the details come later, and must be arranged when the principle is secured. A man has the right to vote because he is a man; but he must possess certain qualifications before he can exercise his right. Let womanhood, as such, cease to be a disqualification; that is the main point. Let the discussion on qualifications follow. Further, if it be urged that women are represented by their husbands, what are we to say about those who have none? In 1861, thirteen years ago, there were three and a-half millions of women in England working for their livelihood - two and a-half millions of these were unmarried, and were, therefore, unrepresented. Is there no pathos in these figures? Two and a-half millions struggling honestly to live, but mute to tell of their wants or their wrongs. Mute, I say, for not one in a thousand has the power of the pen. And this is not the worst. Oh, friends! below these, pressed down there by the terrible struggle for existence, there is a lower depth yet, tenanted by thousands of whom it is not here my province to speak - thousands, from whom a bitter wail goes up, to which men's ears are deaf. Surely, women need representation - surely, there are grievances and wrongs of women which can only be done away by those whom women send to Parliament as their representatives. It is natural that men should not desire that many of these laws should be altered. In the first place, it is impossible they should understand how hardly they press on women; only those who wear it, says the proverb, 'know where the shoe pinches.' And, in the second place, the holders of a monopoly generally object to have their monopoly interfered with. They can't imagine what in the world these outsiders want pressing in upon their special domains. The nobleman cannot understand why the peasant should object to the Game Laws;[29] it is so unreasonable of him. The farmer cannot make out why the labourer should not attend quietly to his hedging and ditching, instead of making all this fuss about a union. The capitalist cannot see the sense of the artisan banding himself with his brethren, instead of going on with his duty, and working hard. Men can't conceive why women do not attend to their household duties instead of fussing about Parliament. Unfortunately, each of these tiresome classes cares very little whether those to whom they are opposed can or cannot understand why they agitate. We may be told continually that we are sufficiently represented; we say that we do not think so, but that we mean to be.

Political power would withdraw women from their proper sphere, and would be a source of domestic annoyance. Their proper sphere? - i.e., the home. This allegation is a very odd one. Men are lawyers, doctors, merchants; every hour of the day is pledged, engrossing speculations stretch the brain, deep questions absorb the mind, great ideas swell in the intellect. Yet men vote. If occupation be a fatal disqualification, let us pass a law that only idle people shall have votes. You will withdraw workers from their various spheres of work, if you allow them to take an interest in politics. For heaven's sake, do not go and take the merchant from the desk, the doctor from the hospital, the lawyer from the court; you will disorganise society - you will withdraw the workers. Do you say it is not so - that the delivery of a vote takes up a very short time at considerable intervals? that a man must have some leisure, and may very well expend it, if he please, in studying politics? that a change of thought is very good for the weary brain? that the alteration of employment is a positive and most valuable relaxation? You are quite right; outside interests are healthy, and prevent private affairs from becoming morbidly engrossing. The study of large problems checks the natural tendency to be absorbed in narrower questions. A man is stronger, healthier, nobler, when, in working hard in trade or in a profession for his home, he does not forget that he is citizen of a mighty nation. I can think of few things more likely to do women real good than anything which would urge them to extend their interests beyond the narrow circle of their homes. Why, men complain that women are bigoted, narrow-minded, prejudiced, impracticable. Wider interests would do much to remedy these defects. If you want your wife to be your toy, or your drudge, you do perhaps wisely in shutting up her ideas within the four walls of your house; but if you want one who will stand at your side through life, in evil report as well as in good, a strong, large-hearted woman, fit to be your comfort in trouble, your counsellor in difficulty, your support in danger, worthy to be the mother of your children, the wise guardian and trainer of your sons and your daughters, then seek to widen women's intellects and to enlarge their hearts by sharing with them your grander plans of life, your deeper thoughts, your keener hopes. Do not keep your brains and your intellects for the strife of politics and the conflicts for success, and give to your homes and to your wives nothing but your condescending carelessness and your thoughtless love. Further, do you look on women as your natural enemies, and suppose they are on the look-out for every chance of running away from their homes and their children? It says very little for you if you hope only to keep women's hearts by chaining their limbs, or limiting their range of action. What is it really worth, this compelled submission—this enforced devotion? Do you acknowledge that you make home life so dull, so wearisome, that you dare not throw open the cage door, lest the captive should escape? Do you confess that your service is so hard a one that she you call your friend is only longing to be free? You do yourselves an injustice, friends; you shame your own characters - you discredit your homes. A happy home, the centre of hopes and fears, the cherished resting place from life's troubles, the sure haven from life's conflicts, the paradise brightened by children's prattle and children's laughter, the heaven where we see God in the faces of the little ones - this home is not a place where women must be chained down lest they should run away. Admitting, however, for argument's sake, the absurd idea that women would neglect their homes if they possessed the franchise, may I ask by what right men restrict women's action to the home? I can understand that, in eastern lands, where the husband rules his wives with despotic authority, and woman is but the plaything and the slave of man, woman's sphere is the home, for the very simple reason that she cannot get outside it. So, in this sense, in the Zoological Gardens, is the den the sphere of the lion and the cage of the eagle. Shut any living creature up, and its prison becomes its sphere. But if the prisoner becomes restless - if nature beats strongly at the captive's heart - if he yearns for the free air and the golden sunshine, you may, indeed, keep him in the sphere you have built for him; but he will break his heart, and will die in your hands. Many women now, educated more highly than they used to be - women with strong brains and loving hearts, are being driven into bitterness and into angry opposition, because their ambition is thwarted at every step, and their eager longings for a fuller life are forced back and crushed. A tree will grow, however you may try to stunt it. You may disfigure it, you may force it into awkward shapes, but grow it will. One would fain hope that it is in thoughtlessness and in ignorance that men try to push women back. Surely they do not appreciate the injury they are doing, both to themselves and to women, if they turn their homes into prison houses and the little children into incumbrances. In the strong, true, woman, there is a tender motherhood which weaker natures cannot reach; but if these women are to be told that domestic cares only are to fill their brains, and the prattle of children to be the only satisfaction of their intellect, you run a terrible risk of making them break free from home and child. Allow them to grow freely, to develop as nature bids them, and they will find room for home-cares in their minds, and the warmest nestling place in their bosom will be the haven of the little child. But if you check, and fret, and carp, at them, you will not succeed in keeping them back, but you will succeed in souring them and in making them hard and bitter. Oh, for the sake of English home life - for the sake of the tender ties of motherhood - for the sake of the common happiness, do not turn into bitter opponents the women who are still anxious to be your friends and your fellow workers. This is no imaginary danger; it is a thundercloud brooding over many English homes. I can scarcely believe that men and women would be so unreasonable as to make the power of voting into a domestic annoyance. Of course, if a married couple want to quarrel, there are sure to be plenty of differences of opinion between them which will give them the proper opportunity. But why should political disagreement be specially fatal to domestic peace? Theology is now a fruitful source of disagreement. If the husband is the free-thinker, he does not suffer, because he does not allow his wife to worry him too far; but if the freethinking is on the side of the wife, matters are apt to become uncomfortable. There is only one way to remedy this difficulty. Let the husband feel, as the wife now does, that between two grown-up people, control of one by the other is an absurdity. Bitterness arises now from disagreement, because the wife who forms her opinion for herself is regarded as a rebel to lawful authority. Remove the authority, which is a tyranny, and people will readily 'agree to differ.' There will possibly be a little more care before marriage about the opinions of the lady wooed, than there is now when the man fancies that he can mould the docile girl into what shape he pleases, and the future happiness of both is marred if the woman happens to be made of bright steel instead of plastic clay. In any case, Parliament is scarcely bound to treat one half of England with injustice, lest the other half should find its authority curtailed.

The last argument, which is to crush us, is the authority of the Bible. Frederick Maurice[30] warned people of the danger they ran when they 'turned the bread of life into stones to cast at their enemies.' Now, passing by the fact that many of us do not consider the Bible as the bread of life in any sense, I would suggest that using it as a pebble to sling at the forehead of Liberty has not, in the past, tended to exalt it, nor is it likely to be more successful in the future. Long ago, a king sat on a beach to warn back the advancing tide. Wave after wave broke into laughter on the strand, and the water rose higher and higher, till it washed the kingly feet, and began to surround the kingly chair. The sea knew no master. And so for centuries has religion stood, with the Bible in her lifted hand; she has warned back each wave of the rising tide of liberty, and each wave has rippled forward regardless of her threats. 'Let every soul be subject to the higher powers,' said the Bible to Cromwell, and Cromwell, though he took off his hat to the Bible, struck down the tyrant who strove to enchain the people. 'Honour the king,' said the Bible to Washington, and Washington defied the king, and founded the American Republic. 'Thou shalt not suffer a witch to live,' said the Bible, and stern law saved the feeble from the Bible-sharpened sword. If a city is withdrawn to serve strange gods, 'thou shalt surely smite the inhabitants of that city with the edge of the sword, destroying it utterly,' said the Bible to Alva, and Alva obediently harried the Netherlands, and the people rose, and fought for their lives, and won. 'Cursed is Canaan: a servant of servants shall he be unto his brethren,' said the Bible from ten thousand pulpits; but men arose, and swore that, Bible or no Bible, the slave should go free. The Bible! why, it has bolstered up every injustice - it has bulwarked every tyranny - it has defended every wrong. With toil and pain and bloodshed have the soldiers of Liberty wrung from the reluctant hands of priests and Bible worshippers every charter of our freedom, every triumph of our cause. Every step in science has been won despite of the Bible; every inch of natural knowledge has been conquered at the sword's point from the realm of the supernatural. From the stake where Bruno[31] stood and died, from the dungeon where Galileo[32] knelt and trembled, a voice has rung out that every advance of science has been struggled against by the Bible and the Church. But take heart, you who cling to your Bibles; as soon as we have gained this one step forward - as soon as it rings through England that women are no longer in subjection, you will be able to claim as the offspring of your Christianity that which, at its birth, you anathematised. Each trophy of advancement, each symbol of triumph, is claimed by the Bibliolator[33] as his as soon as it becomes popular. You will be able to find in your Bibles a sanction for the free development of womanhood, even as you have found room in the six days of Genesis for the vast æons of geology, and space in the petty firmament of Moses for the mighty facts of astronomy. The Bible is claimed as the true parent of modern freedom, as the striker-off of the chains of the slave, the guardian of the feeble from the tyranny of the strong. It is the spirit of Christianity has done it all, you say; when the letter said 'kill,' it meant 'preserve;' when the letter said 'obey,' it meant 'resist;' when the letter said 'enslave,' it meant 'set free.' So take courage, ye worshippers of a book; your idol will be shattered once more, but it can once more be re-mended; it will fall once more before the trumpet-blast of Freedom, but once more it can be raised. We mean to set woman free; free to follow the guiding hand of Nature; free to fulfil every fair capability of her being; free to develop every noble intellectual power, and every passionate longing of her heart; free to expand in every direction; free to grow, to strengthen, and to rise. Little care we whether or not our work square with the rules of an old eastern civilisation; let those who are anxious about it see to that. Our work need not in itself trench on religion; but if Religion and the Bible grapple with us, and try to stop and destroy us, then Religion and the Bible must either stand aside, or else they must go down.

One by one I have faced the only arguments against the extension of the franchise to women with which I am acquainted. You yourselves must judge how far these arguments are valid, and on which side right and justice rest. I would add that I feel sure that, when the matter is fairly placed before them, most men will sympathise with, and assist our cause. Some noble and brave men have come forward to join our ranks already, and speak boldly for woman's cause, and work faithfully for its triumph. The mass of men only need to study our claims in order to accept them. They have been reared to regard themselves as our natural superiors; small blame to them that they take the upper seats. Kind and gentle as many of them are, working hard for wife and children, thinking much of women and loving them well, it cannot be expected that they should readily understand that their relations to the weaker sex are founded on an injustice. But if they want to see how false is their idea of peace, and how misled they are when they think women's position satisfactory, let them go out and see what the laws are where the power they give is wielded by brutality and tyranny. Let them try to imagine what women suffer who are too weak and timid to resist the strength under whose remorseless exercise they writhe in vain; let them try to appreciate the sharper agony of those whose bolder hearts and stronger natures defy their tyrants, and break, at whatever cost, their chains. Laws must be tested by their working; these laws which make the woman the helpless servant of man are not enforced in happy homes. But they exist, and elsewhere they are used.

Injustice is never good; it is never even safe. There is a higher life before us, a nobler ideal of marriage union, a fairer development of individual natures, a surer hope of wider happiness. Liberty for every human being, equality before the law for all in public and in private, fraternity of men and women in peaceful friendship, these are the promise of the dawning day. Co-workers in every noble labour, co-partners in every righteous project, co-soldiers in every just cause, men and women in the time to come shall labour, think, and struggle side by side. The man shall bring his greater strength and more sustained determination, the woman her quicker judgment and purer heart, till man shall grow tenderer, and woman stronger, man more pure, and woman more brave and free. Till at last, generations hence, the race shall develop into a strength and a beauty at present unimagined, and men and women shall walk this fair earth hand-in-hand, diverse yet truly one, set each to each - 'as perfect music unto noble words.'

NB. In the debate which followed this lecture, exception was taken by some of the speakers to the introduction of the religious question, and it was suggested that in attacking the Bible, I had thrown down an apple of discord. I would point out that the raising of this question was not of my doing. Had the speakers known a little more of the subject, they would have been aware that the authority of the Bible is constantly brought forward as an argument against women's rights, and had I avoided meeting this argument, I should have left out a link in my chain. The Bible has so great an influence in this country, that its dictum to the contrary is sufficient to destroy, in most minds, the most logical arguments. Had I wished to impeach the Bible as a whole, I should have made a very different attack upon it; but, in this lecture, nothing more was needed than to state forcibly that, so far as it touched on the subject, the Bible must be set aside, and a few historical parallels were added for the comfort of both friends and foes. The advocates of women's rights have not the least desire to mix up the religious question with the political agitation; but if our opponents fling the Bible at our heads, are we forbidden to turn it aside by lifting against it the shield of free-thought?

NOTES

NOTES

1. Marcel Proust was a French novelist, critic, and essayist known for his monumental novel *À la recherche du temps perdu* (*In Search of Lost Time* or in an earlier translation, *Remembrance of Things Past*). This monumental work was published in seven parts between 1913 and 1927. Proust had struggled with ill health from childhood and spent the last three years of his life mostly confined to his bedroom, sleeping during the day and working at night to complete his novel.

2. Ian Paul Livingston, Baron Livingston of Parkhead (b. 1964) is a Scottish businessman and a Conservative member of the House of Lords. He previously served as Minister of State for Trade and Investment. He joined BT Group as Finance Director and was promoted to the role of CEO, BT Retail in 2005. He replaced Ben Verwaayen as Group CEO in June 2008.

3. The BT Operating Committee was the executive team ultimately responsible for running BT Group. It has since been replaced by the BT Executive Committee (ExCo). ExCo members are the BT Chief Executive, BT Chief Financial Officer, BT HR Director, Chief Strategy and Transformation Officer, Regulatory Director, Corporate Affairs Director, General Counsel and the Chief Executive Officers (CEOs) of Consumer, Enterprise, Global Services, and Technology, Service and Operations (TSO).

4. The artist Martin Firrell hosted a dinner to discuss senior women's experience of power. The aim was to identify a commonality, if any existed, between the way different women regard, hold, and use power. The attendees included Liv Garfield, Inga Beale (then CEO, Lloyd's of London) and Clare Short (Secretary of State for International Development 1997-2003). The dinner took place on 25 June 2018 at the artist's home in Soho.

5. The use of all-women shortlists is an affirmative action practice intended to increase the proportion of female Members of Parliament in the United Kingdom. As the name suggests, the practice identifies constituencies where all candidates for selection and election are women. Only the Labour Party and Liberal

NOTES

Democrats currently use all-women shortlists. In the 1990s, women constituted less than 10% of MPs in the House of Commons of the UK Parliament. Political parties used various strategies in an attempt to increase female representation, including motivating women to stand and encouraging constituency associations to select them, and providing special training for potential female candidates. For the 1992 general election, the Labour Party had a policy of ensuring there was at least one woman candidate on each of its shortlists, however few of these women were successful in being selected in winnable seats (seats within a 6% swing). Following polling that suggested women were less likely to vote Labour than men, the party introduced all-women shortlists at the Labour Party's 1993 annual conference.

6. The Hampton-Alexander Review is an independent review body working to increase the number of women on FTSE 350 boards. The Review adopts a voluntary business-led approach, with a dual focus of improving women's representation at board level and also in leadership roles two layers below the board. The Review covers 23,000 leadership roles across all sectors of British business. It is chaired by Sir Philip Hampton and led by its CEO Denise Wilson OBE.

7. The Theosophical Society was founded by the Russian occultist Helena Petrovna Blavatsky in New York City in 1875. The society aims to explore the interconnectedness of all life, the universal wisdoms held in ancient religions and myths, and the potential latent in human beings.

8. The Irish Home Rule movement campaigned for self-government for Ireland. It was the dominant political movement of Irish nationalism from 1870 to the end of World War I. The Indian self-rule movement was a mass movement involving diverse sections of society. Although its basic ideology was anti-colonial, the movement championed independent capitalist economic development coupled with a secular, democratic, republican and civil-libertarian political structure.

NOTES

9. Banaras Hindu University, formerly Central Hindu College, is a public central university located in Varanasi, Uttar Pradesh. It was established in 1916 by Madan Mohan Malaviya and Annie Besant. With over 30,000 students residing in campus, it is the largest residential university in Asia.

10. The National Secular Society is a British campaigning organisation that promotes secularism and the separation of church and state. It maintains that no one should gain advantage or disadvantage because of their religion or lack of it. It was founded by the English political activist and atheist, Charles Bradlaugh in 1866.

11. *The Fruits of Philosophy: or The Private Companion of Young Married People* was a relatively obscure publication providing elementary (but not entirely accurate) contraceptive information. The pamphlet became notorious in 1876 when a Bristol bookseller, Henry Cook, was sentenced to two years' hard labour for selling it. Bradlaugh and Besant republished the pamphlet bringing it up-to-date with medical footnotes by Dr George Drysdale. There was nothing in the pamphlet that was unknown to medical practitioners or which had not been published before. The issue was that it was being published at a price (sixpence) that made it available to ordinary working people. Bradlaugh and Besant were arrested on Thursday 5 April 1877 and charged under the Obscene Publications Act 1857. The case came to court on 18 June, becoming a cause celebre. Besant and Bradlaugh defended themselves, which was unusual enough but unprecedented for a woman in the 1870s. Besant and Bradlaugh were found guilty but the judgement was eventually overturned on a technicality.

12. The matchgirls' strike of 1888 was an industrial action by the women and teenage girls working at the Bryant & May match factory in Bow, London. The strike was caused by the poor working conditions in the match factory, including 14-hour work days, poor pay, excessive fines, and severe health complications associated with white phosphorus. Approximately 1,400 women and girls withdrew their labour. On 6 July, 100 of the striking women went to see Annie Besant to ask for

her assistance. It has often been said that she started or led the strike but this is not the case. She knew nothing about it until the women's visit and was at first dismayed by the rashness of the action they had taken and by the number of women who were now out of work with no means of support. Besant supported the striking women in meetings with the Bryant and May management. On 16 July, new terms of employment were agreed, answering the women's grievances and, importantly, agreeing that meals would be taken in a separate room, where the food would not be contaminated with phosphorus.

13. The Fabian Society is a British socialist organisation that aims to advance the principles of democratic socialism via gradualist and reformist action in democracies, rather than by revolutionary overthrow. The Fabian Society has been a significant force in British politics as one of the founding organisations of the Labour Representation Committee in 1900, and as a major influence on the Labour Party, which grew from it. Members of the Fabian Society have included political leaders from countries formerly part of the British Empire, such as Jawaharlal Nehru, who adopted Fabian principles as part of their own political ideologies. In 1895, the Fabian Society founded the London School of Economics and Political Science, the LSE.

14. The Social Democratic Federation was Britain's first organised socialist political party. The British Marxist movement effectively began in 1880 when a businessman named Henry M. Hyndman read Karl Marx's Communist Manifesto. Hyndman sought out Marx, then an exile living not far from his home. Hyndman decided to start a new political organisation which he called the Democratic Federation. In 1884 the Democratic Federation was transformed into the Social Democratic Federation (SDF) when the group adopted an explicitly socialist platform. The Federation was strongly opposed to the Liberal Party which then claimed to represent the labour movement in parliament. The programme of the SDF was strongly progressive, calling for (amongst other measures) a 48-hour working week, the abolition of child labour, compulsory, free, secular

education, equality for women, and the nationalisation of the means of production, distribution, and exchange by a democratic state.

15. Helena Petrovna Blavatsky (1831-1891) was a Russian occultist, philosopher, and author who co-founded the Theosophical Society in 1875. She gained an international following as theosophy's leading theoretician. In 1877, she published *Isis Unveiled*, a book outlining her theosophical world view. She described Theosophy as 'the synthesis of science, religion and philosophy', explaining that it was, in effect, a revival of a much earlier 'Ancient Wisdom' underpinning all world religions. In 1880 she moved to India along with the society's co-founder Henry Steel Olcott. Although opposed by the British administration, theosophy spread rapidly in India. In 1885, Blavatsky returned to Europe in poor health, establishing the Blavatsky Lodge in London. She published *The Secret Doctrine* in 1888, a commentary on what she claimed were ancient Tibetan manuscripts. She published two further books - *The Key to Theosophy* and *The Voice of the Silence*. She died of influenza in 1891.

16. Central Hindu School, formerly known as Central Hindu College, was founded by Annie Besant in July 1898, with Dr. Arthur Richardson, a science graduate from England as the principal. The school would later form the nucleus of Banaras Hindu University, established in 1916.

17. The Hyderabad (Sind) National Collegiate Board, or HSNC Board, is an Indian non-profit organisation established by the Sindhi Community in 1922. It was relocated to Mumbai after Partition with Pakistan in 1947. It is one of the oldest educational trusts in India and currently administers 27 institutes.

18. Co-Freemasonry is a form of Freemasonry which admits both men and women. It began in France in the 1890s with the formation of *Le Droit Humain* and is now an international movement represented by several Co-Freemasonic administrations throughout the world. Most male-only Masonic Lodges do not recognise Co-Freemasonry, regarding it as irregular, or clandestine.

NOTES

19. The Home Rule League (1873-1882), sometimes called the Home Rule Party or the Home Rule Confederation, was a political party which campaigned for home rule for Ireland within the United Kingdom of Great Britain and Ireland, until it was replaced by the Irish Parliamentary Party.

20. Mary Somerville (née Fairfax, 1780-1872), was a Scottish science writer and polymath. She studied mathematics and astronomy, and was jointly nominated with Caroline Herschel as the first female member of the Royal Astronomical Society. When John Stuart Mill, the philosopher and economist, organised a massive petition to parliament to give women the right to vote, Somerville's signature was the first on the petition.

21. Mary Ann Evans adopted the pen name George Eliot to avoid being stereotyped as a female author limited to writing lighthearted romances. She also wanted to have her fiction judged separately from her already extensive and widely known work as an editor and critic. Another factor in her use of a pen name may have been a desire to shield her private life from public scrutiny.

22. Frances Power Cobbe (1822-1904) was an Irish writer, social reformer, anti-vivisection activist, and leading women's suffrage campaigner. She founded a number of animal advocacy groups, including the National Anti-Vivisection Society (NAVS) in 1875, and the British Union for the Abolition of Vivisection (BUAV) in 1898, and was a member of the executive council of the London National Society for Women's Suffrage.

23. Harriet Martineau (1802-1876) was a British social theorist and Liberal writer, often cited as the first female sociologist. She wrote many books and a multitude of essays from a sociological, holistic, religious, domestic, and perhaps most controversially of all, feminine perspective.

24. John Stuart Mill (1806-1873) was a British philosopher, political economist and civil servant. One of the most influential thinkers in

the history of classical liberalism, he contributed widely to social theory, political theory, and political economy. Mill was a proponent of utilitarianism, an ethical theory developed by the philosopher and social reformer, Jeremy Bentham. Mill was a member of the Liberal Party and the second Member of Parliament to call for women's suffrage after Henry Hunt.

25. The Bastille was a fortress in Paris, known formally as the Bastille Saint-Antoine. It played an important role in the internal conflicts of France and for most of its history was used as a state prison by the kings of France. It was stormed by a crowd on 14 July 1789, in the French Revolution, becoming an important symbol for the French Republican movement. It was later demolished and replaced by the Place de la Bastille.

26. Millicent Garrett Fawcett (1847-1929), was an English political leader, activist and writer known primarily as a campaigner for women's suffrage. As a suffragist, she took a moderate line on women's rights, but campaigned tirelessly. In 1897 she became the president of the National Union of Women's Suffrage Societies (NUWSS). She focused strongly on improving women's chances of higher education. She served as a governor of Bedford College, London (now Royal Holloway) and co-founded Newnham College, Cambridge in 1875. 'I cannot say I became a suffragist,' she later wrote. 'I always was one, from the time I was old enough to think at all about the principles of representative government.'

27. Jacob Bright (1821-1899) was a British Liberal politician. He was born at Green Bank near Rochdale, Lancashire, the fourth child of Jacob Bright and Martha Wood. His father was a Quaker and had established a cotton-spinning business at Fieldhouse. His elder brother, John Bright, was a radical politician, and his sister, Priscilla Bright McLaren, campaigned for women's rights. Bright became involved in radical politics and supported Chartism. He was the first mayor of Rochdale on the town's incorporation as a municipal borough. He stood for election in 1865 in Manchester. Although unsuccessful on his first attempt, he won a by-election in 1867. The

election was notable because the Scottish suffragist Lilly Maxwell voted for Bright. This vote by a woman was later invalidated. As a Member of Parliament, Bright was considered an 'advanced radical'. He was a peace campaigner and supported women's suffrage.

28. Moncure Daniel Conway (1832-1907) was an American abolitionist minister. He led freethinkers in London's South Place Chapel, now Conway Hall. In 1868 Conway was one of four speakers at the first open public meeting in support of women's suffrage in Great Britain.

29. Under William the Conqueror, it was as great a crime to kill one of the king's deer as to kill one of his subjects. A certain rank and standing, or the possession of a certain amount of property, were vital qualifications for acquiring the right of pursuing and killing game. Game laws such as the British Night Poaching Act 1828 and Game Act 1831, both still in force in modified form, enacted savage penalties for poaching.

30. John Frederick Denison Maurice (1805-1872) was an English Anglican theologian, a prolific author, and one of the founders of Christian socialism. In 1847, Maurice and 'most of his brother-professors' at King's College formed a Committee on Education for the education of governesses. This committee joined a scheme for establishing a College for Women that resulted in the founding of Queen's College. Maurice was its first principal. The college was 'empowered to grant certificates of qualification to governesses' and 'to open classes in all branches of female education'.

31. Giordano Bruno, born Filippo Bruno, (1548-1600) was an Italian Dominican friar, philosopher, mathematician, poet, cosmological theorist, and Hermetic occultist. He is known for his cosmological theories, which extended the then-novel Copernican model. He proposed that the stars were distant suns surrounded by their own planets, and he raised the possibility that these planets might foster life of their own, a philosophical position known as cosmic pluralism. He also insisted that the universe is infinite and could have no 'centre'. Bruno was tried for heresy by the Roman Inquisition on

charges of denying several core Catholic doctrines, including eternal damnation, the Trinity, the divinity of Christ, the virginity of Mary, and transubstantiation. The Inquisition found him guilty and he was burned at the stake in Rome's Campo de' Fiori in 1600.

32. Galileo Galilei (1564-1642) was an astronomer, physicist and engineer. His championship of heliocentrism and Copernicanism was controversial during his lifetime. He met with opposition from astronomers, who doubted heliocentrism because of the absence of an observed stellar parallax. The matter was investigated by the Roman Inquisition in 1615, which concluded that heliocentrism was 'foolish and absurd in philosophy, and formally heretical since it explicitly contradicts in many places the sense of Holy Scripture'. Galileo later defended his views in Dialogue Concerning the Two Chief World Systems (1632), which appeared to attack Pope Urban VIII and thus alienated him and the Jesuits, who had both supported Galileo up until this point. He was tried by the Inquisition, found 'vehemently suspect of heresy', and forced to recant. He spent the rest of his life under house arrest.

33. In Christianity, bibliolatry denotes extreme devotion to the Bible or to the idea that the Bible is entirely without error (biblical inerrancy). Supporters of biblical inerrancy point to passages (such as 2 Timothy 3:16–17) interpreted to mean that the Bible, as received, is a complete source of what must be known about God. Critics of this view call it a form of idolatry, pointing to verses (such as John 5:39–40) to indicate that Christ asked humanity to relate to God directly.

MARTIN FIRRELL

The public artist Martin Firrell uses text in public space to promote debate. The more people think about, question and debate a topic, the more likely it becomes that change will occur.

Firrell uses language to engage directly with the public, promoting constructive dialogues, usually about marginalisation, equality and more equitable social organisation, with the aim of making the world more humane. His work has been summarised as 'art as debate'.

Socialart.work is a mass public art project created by Martin Firrell calling for greater social justice. It aims to create debate about power and its abuse, feminism, women's equality and gender, alternative forms of economic and social organisation, black power, counter-culture, and solidarity between people of different backgrounds and ethnicities.

The project includes posters, publications and events supported in 2018-19 by the digital media company Clear Channel UK.

Martin Firrell has been described in the Guardian as 'one of the capital's most influential public artists'.

More information about this project can be found at www.socialart.work. More information about the artist can be found at Wikipedia.

www.ingramcontent.com/pod-product-compliance
Lightning Source LLC
Chambersburg PA
CBHW020302030426
42336CB00010B/866